"An excellent resource for students, educators and families. As a middle school counselor, I will definitely use this as a tool to help our students succeed in the area of executive functioning!"

—**Lisa Koenecke**, Wisconsin School Counselor Association President

"I think it would be an invaluable resource for executive skills coaches and for teachers developing executive skills seminars for groups of students. The activities and exercises are versatile enough that they could be used with individual students or with groups of students—and coaches and seminar leaders could easily pick and choose which executive skills to emphasize and which exercises to use."

—**Peg Dawson, EdD**, psychologist and author of several books on executive skills, including *Smart but Scattered*

"Many teens struggle with executive functioning challenges, especially those with attention deficit/hyperactivity disorder (ADHD), learning disabilities, high functioning autism, or other conditions. This workbook gives these teens (and their parents) strategies to improve their executive functions, which means they can develop skills to improve their lives."

—**Dr. Kenny Handelman**, author of *Attention Difference Disorder*

the executive functioning workbook for teens

help for unprepared, late & scattered teens

SHARON A. HANSEN, MSE, NBCT

Instant Help Books
An Imprint of New Harbinger Publications, Inc.

Publisher's Note

Distributed in Canada by Raincoast Books

Copyright © 2013 by Sharon Hansen
     Instant Help Books
     An Imprint of New Harbinger Publications, Inc.
     5674 Shattuck Avenue
     Oakland, CA 94609
     www.newharbinger.com

INSTANT HELP, the Clock Logo, and NEW HARBINGER are trademarks of New Harbinger Publications, Inc.

Cover design by Amy Shoup
Acquired by Tesilya Hanauer
Edited by Will DeRooy

Activity 3, "Defeating Your Beast," adapted from THERE'S A MONSTER IN MY CLOSET activity, copyright © 2012 Carolyn Berger. Used with permission.

Library of Congress Cataloging-in-Publication Data

Hansen, Sharon A.
 The executive functioning workbook for teens : help for unprepared, late, and scattered teens / Sharon A. Hansen, MSE, NBCT.
  pages cm
 Audience: Age 14-18
 ISBN 978-1-60882-656-8 (pbk. : alk. paper) -- ISBN 978-1-60882-657-5 (pdf e-book) -- ISBN 978-1-60882-658-2 (epub) 1. Executive ability in adolescence--Juvenile literature. 2. Self-management (Psychology) for teenagers--Juvenile literature. 3. Self-control in adolescence--Juvenile literature. 4. Attention in adolescence--Juvenile literature. I. Title.
 BF723.E93H36 2013
 155.5'19--dc23
     2013011601

Printed in the United States of America

23 22 21

20 19 18 17 16 15

To my husband Steve: Thanks for being my rock and believing in me, even when I sometimes don't.

To my daughter Kylie: Be proud of who you are. I am proud to be the mother of such a strong young woman,

To my son Christopher, the inspiration for this book: I always knew you could do it, and you did. I am proud of the amazing young man you have turned out to be. Now, go get the world!

contents

for teens

Just as we all have different fingerprints, we all have very different brains. Some people's brains are very good at remembering things. Other people's brains are incredibly creative. Still other people's brains are extremely organized. Whatever kind of brain you have, it's yours and you need to learn how to work *with* it, instead of against it.

Do you ever feel as though other teens understand things more easily than you do? Do others your age seem to "have it together," while *you* sometimes feel as though you'd lose your head if it weren't attached to your body?

At times, you may have felt lost, confused, unprepared, or scattered. This can be a normal part of growing up. However, for some teens, these feelings indicate weakness in executive functioning.

Executive functioning is a set of skills that include self-understanding, organizational skill, time management ability, emotion control, behavior control, flexibility, initiative, attention, working memory, and persistence. A person may have a weakness in any one of these areas or multiple areas. What does weakness in executive functioning look like, sound like, and feel like? Well, that depends.

A teen with a weakness in organizational skill may have a very hard time keeping his binder or locker in order. Another teen with a weakness in working memory may not be able to remember that she has homework. Still another teen with a weakness in behavior control may blurt things out in the middle of class. Sound familiar? If so, this book may prove very helpful.

While this book is meant for you to use on your own, I highly encourage you to find an adult whom you trust who can help you as needed. Ideally, this person should be your parent, but it doesn't have to be. It might be a trusted teacher or your school counselor. The more you practice the activities in this book, the better your skills will become; and a helpful adult may be able to give you valuable pointers.

Our goal as humans should be to effectively manage our lives, make positive decisions, and move ourselves toward a bright and rewarding future. I hope that you find the activities in this book helpful in making that future come true for you.

Best of luck!

Sharon Hansen

When my son Chris was born, I envisioned that he would be intelligent, well-behaved, and a good student. Now a high school graduate, Chris is indeed very intelligent, and most of the time he is well-behaved. However, in school, there were times his grades were less than stellar.

Throughout school, Chris had a hard time completing homework, remembering to bring things home, and taking any kind of interest in school. By fifth grade, neuropsychological testing indicated that he had weaknesses in organizational skill, processing speed, and working memory—abilities that contribute to what is known as *executive functioning*.

Executive functioning is a set of skills that help people organize, plan, and control their life to make sure things get done. Teens who have weakness in executive functioning have a hard time starting tasks, sustaining effort, and finishing what they start.

Chris is not less smart than other students his age; his brain simply does not work the same as that of a teen who is a stellar student. Just as some people are short and some are tall, some people have better executive skills than others do. If your child has trouble with tasks that require executive skills, she is not "abnormal"; she is just a different kind of normal.

In many teens, the area of the brain where most executive functioning takes place—the prefrontal cortex—is still developing. The most recent brain research indicates that this pre-frontal cortex is not completely developed until a young person is in his or her mid- to late twenties. This is important, because it means that there are many things you can do to help improve your child's executive skills. Just as it took your child lots of practice before he was able to walk, talk, ride a bike, or do anything else well, he can develop his executive skills through practice.

Your child may be strong in some areas of executive functioning, but weaker in others. The first activity in this book will help gauge your child's ability in different areas. Once you and your child know her strengths and weaknesses, you can help her choose which skills to work on.

While the activities in this book can help your child improve his executive skills, they must be repeated several times before they "sink in" and become habits. For most people, it takes about twenty-eight days to learn a new habit. For teens who have difficulty with tasks that require executive skills, it can take twice or three times as long. As well as a struggle for these teens themselves, this can be frustrating for anyone trying to help them (you, for example). Therefore, while this book is meant for teens to use on their own, I strongly encourage you to participate in the activities as much as possible and to act as your child's "executive skills coach" until he is able to consistently perform the tasks expected of him. With this "scaffolding" in place, your child is much more likely to be successful.

I wish you luck on your journey, and although you may at times become frustrated in your efforts to support your child's development, please remember to be gentle with your child.

Sharon Hansen

executive skills
self-assessment

for you to know

Executive function disorder (EFD) is a term that applies to people who have a hard time performing certain tasks required to carry out their daily responsibilities. These include, but are not limited to, analyzing, organizing, deciding, and planning. At school, teens with EFD may have difficulty getting assignments done and turned in on time; keeping their folders, binders, and lockers organized; and managing their time while resisting distractions. At home, teens with EFD may have difficulty handling their emotions, following a series of directions, or keeping their room clean.

Just as some people are short and some are tall, some people have better executive skills than others do. You're not "abnormal" if you have EFD; you're just a different kind of normal. It may be better to think of "average" as opposed to "normal." Just as a grade of C is average—middle of the range—you can think of most teens as having average brains.

The assessment that follows will allow you to determine your areas of strength and weakness in executive functioning. You can then use this information to plan which sections of the book to work through first. After tackling your weakest skills, you can proceed to those areas that don't need quite as much attention. The better your executive skills, the more effective you'll be in life.

for you to do

Read each of the following statements. Circle those that are true for you, based on what you know about yourself or have heard from other people. (The areas are numbered for now but will be identified shortly.)

Area 1

- I hurry through tasks just to get them done.

- I dislike tasks or games that require the use of problem-solving skills.

- I need to have directions repeated.

- People have told me that I am unaware of how my behavior affects others.

Area 2

- I have a hard time remembering to bring home items needed to complete my assignments.

- I have a hard time finding my completed assignments.

- I have a hard time keeping my room, backpack, locker, or desk clean and orderly.

- I have a hard time finding needed items on a regular basis.

Area 3

- I have a hard time starting assignments or chores early so that they get done on time.

- I have a hard time fitting new events into my schedule.

- I have a hard time accurately estimating how long something will take to complete.

- I often miss due dates or deadlines for assignments or tasks.

Area 4

- I have frequent temper tantrums.
- I feel nervous more often than others my age do.
- I have a hard time controlling my angry feelings.
- I get upset by small issues.

Area 5

- I interrupt conversations.
- People have told me that I make inappropriate comments or remarks.
- I start tasks without waiting for or reading all the instructions.
- I blurt out answers in class without being called on by the teacher.

Area 6

- I have a hard time handling unplanned changes in a schedule.
- I have trouble moving from class to class or transitioning from school to home at the end of the day.
- I give up on a task if my first attempt is not successful.
- I have a hard time asking for help if something is not clear.

Area 7

- I have a hard time starting tasks without being told.
- I need reminders to finish tasks like chores or homework.
- I need reminders to follow classroom or house rules.
- I have a hard time moving from one task to another.

Area 8

- I have a hard time completing tasks, especially if they get difficult.
- I feel overwhelmed by large assignments or projects.
- I have a hard time ignoring small distractions in my environment.
- I talk to nearby people instead of working on a task.

Area 9

- I have a hard time remembering a verbal list of three or more things to do.
- I forget to hand in all my homework.
- I have a hard time remembering to bring home items that I need to complete work.
- I answer only the first part of a multiple-part question.

Area 10

- I have a hard time returning to a task if I am interrupted while doing it.
- I have a hard time staying "on task" if the task is boring to me.
- I am easily distracted while trying to focus on work.
- I have a hard time setting goals in school or at home.

If you circled more than two statements out of any group of four, you may have weakness in that particular area of executive functioning. For every area, there are three activities in this book that can help you improve your skills:

Area 1—Self-Understanding (the ability to assess how well you understand yourself and how you do things): Activities 2, 3, and 4

Area 2—Organizational Skill (the ability to establish and maintain order and keep track of things): Activities 5, 6, and 7

Area 3—Time Management Ability (the ability to accurately estimate how long a task will take and to make efficient use of time): Activities 8, 9, and 10

Area 4—Emotion Control (the ability to stay calm even when faced with situations that can cause you to get upset, angry, sad, or frustrated): Activities 11, 12, and 13

Area 5—Behavior Control (the ability to stop yourself from doing things you shouldn't): Activities 14, 15, and 16

Area 6—Flexibility (the ability to make changes in your behavior or schedule): Activities 17, 18, and 19

Area 7—Initiative (the ability to start projects or tasks without having someone tell you to): Activities 20, 21, and 22

Area 8—Attention (the ability to stay focused on a task that is uninteresting to you, especially with distractions): Activities 23, 24, and 25

Area 9—Working Memory (the ability to keep certain information in mind in order to complete a task): Activities 26, 27, and 28

Area 10—Persistence (the ability to stick with a boring task from start to finish): Activities 29, 30, and 31 (Activity 31 is a concluding activity that works best after you've completed at least several other activities.)

more to do

Figuring out where to start improving your executive skills can be hard. You may find it very helpful to take a little time right now to write a plan for how you'll use this book.

In doing the assessment on the previous pages, you may have noticed that you're weaker in some areas of executive functioning than in others. Rank the areas from your assessment from weakest to strongest. That is, first list any areas in which you circled all four statements, then those in which you circled three, and so on. Then start working on the activities for number one and work your way to number ten.

1. _____

2. _____

3. _____

4. _____

5. _____

6. _____

7. _____

8. _____

9. _____

10. _____

seeing yourself 2

for you to know

One of the tricky things about weakness in executive functioning is that if you have it, you can't always see it. Sometimes you need to have others reflect back to you, like a mirror, what problems they see you having. Knowing exactly what the problem is can be one of the most important steps in finding a solution.

Jamal, fourteen, didn't understand why the adults in his life were always on his case. His teachers and parents were always yelling at him to do this and do that. According to Jamal, he did fine in school. He failed a class only occasionally. He couldn't see that he was just not putting real effort into his schoolwork and his chores and that this was a problem.

One day, Jamal's mom and dad sat him down and tried to explain their concerns to him. They said that he was a smart boy, but he was working far below his ability. They told him that he needed to straighten up and do better in school and with his chores. At first, Jamal didn't buy into the "picture" his parents presented to him. However, over the following days, he began to think that maybe his parents were right. He noticed that his teachers treated him differently than the students who were better at following directions and turning in their homework.

Jamal decided to try a little experiment. For the next three days, he made an effort to complete his homework on time and get it turned in. He worked very hard to pay attention in class and ignore the distractions around him. He listened very carefully to what his parents told him, and he wrote down what he needed to do. Pretty soon, he noticed that the adults in his life started to act differently toward him. They were more patient with him and were willing to take the time to help him with things he didn't understand. Because of this, Jamal worked harder at these things until they became habits.

for you to do

In the top part of the following box, use words or pictures to describe how you see yourself. Include both your good points and your bad points. In the bottom part, use words or pictures to describe how other people—your parents, teachers, friends, and siblings—see you. Again, put in both good and bad points.

How I see myself:

How others see me:

more to do

Answer the following questions about what you wrote or drew in the previous exercise.

How is your description or picture of how you see yourself similar to your description or picture of how others see you?

_____

_____

How is your description or picture of how you see yourself different from the description or picture of how others see you?

_____

_____

What do you think are the reasons for these differences?

_____

_____

Which description or picture do you think is more like the "real" you? (Circle your answer.)

How I See Myself   How Others See Me

How can you combine the good things from both descriptions or pictures (or change the bad things) to start creating a new "you" who's better at doing what you need to do and being the person both you and others want you to be?

_____

_____

3   defeating your "beast"

for you to know

Many teens whose executive skills are not so great begin to think negatively about themselves. They start to believe that their weaknesses make them not as good as other people. Keeping *who you are as a person* separate from your weaknesses will help you *externalize* the problem (separate it from yourself) and work on it without letting it negatively affect your self-esteem.

As we saw in activity 2, it can be difficult to know where your weaknesses are. Even when you've identified your areas of weakness, you may feel as though you don't have any chance of improving in these areas, but you *do*. Strengthening your executive skills will allow you to become better at almost anything you do.

Sometimes it helps to take a step back from yourself and look at your situation from the outside, rather than from the inside. While this can be hard to do, once you know how to do it, you'll become much better at determining what you can control and what you can't. Then you can take steps to make changes so that your life can move in a positive direction.

for you to do

In the first box, write the executive skill you need to work on the most. (See activity 1 for a reminder of the ten executive functioning areas.) In the second box, write down a real creature that used to scare you or maybe still does. After filling in these boxes, draw a picture of a "beast" that somehow symbolizes both your executive skill limitations and the creature you're afraid of.

The executive skill that I need to work on the most:	Something that I used to be, or still am, afraid of:

A picture of a "beast" that symbolizes both of the above:

more to do

Imagining your weakness as a "beast" that comes around from time to time, rather than as a part of you or something inside you, helps you realize that you can take action to defeat it or reduce its impact on your life.

Answer the following questions about the "beast" you drew.

What does this "beast" do to cause chaos in your life?

_____

What makes this "beast" happy?

_____

What types of tricks does this "beast" use to get its way?

_____

How do you feel about the chaos this "beast" causes?

_____

What makes this "beast" unhappy?

_____

How can you keep this "beast" from taking over your life?

_____

What steps can you take to prevent this "beast" from coming back?

_____

If you struggle with defeating this "beast," who can you connect with for some assistance?

_____

for you to know

Most often, teens with weakness in executive functioning don't think about doing their best on work. Many will rush through tasks just to get them finished. Being able to slow down will help you put more effort into the things you do.

In school, Johanna, sixteen, would hurry through assignments and make careless mistakes. At home, she completed chores so quickly that she often didn't do a very good job on them. This behavior frustrated Johanna's parents, but she didn't notice. She thought she was doing fine.

Finally, after many bad grades, Johanna's teachers and parents decided to sit down with her. They explained how they saw her rushing to get things finished and suggested that this was a big factor in how well she did her schoolwork and chores. Johanna admitted that maybe they were right, and after that she worked hard at slowing herself down. She noticed that when she took her time with pretty much any task, she did a much better job. As a result, her parents were happier with the way she did chores, and her teachers were happier with the work she turned in. Johanna was more contented now that her parents and teachers were happier, and she was glad that her grades had improved.

for you to do

The acronym/acrostic SLOW is a way for you to remember to slow down and take your time when doing a task.

S—Stop.

L—Listen to suggestions.

O—Observe someone doing the task correctly.

W—Work hard to complete the task as shown.

In the chart that follows, identify some tasks you may often do too quickly.

Tasks Others Have Told Me I Rush Through	
At School	At Home
Example: **spelling tests**	Example: **doing the dishes**

Think about which of the tasks you listed would be good ones to use SLOW with. When can you listen to suggestions and follow someone's example?

more to do

Pick one of the tasks you listed in the previous exercise that you do on a regular basis, and write it in the following space.

_____

The next time you do this task, figure out how long it takes you: do the task the way you normally do it, but note your starting time and your finishing time.

Starting time: _____ Finishing time: _____ How long it took: _____

Rate the quality of your performance on the task using a scale of 1 to 10 (1 = poor; 10 = great). Circle your rating.

1   2   3   4   5   6   7   8   9   10

Now, have your parent or teacher rate the quality of your performance on the task using the same scale. Circle your parent or teacher's rating.

1   2   3   4   5   6   7   8   9   10

Discuss with your parent or teacher in what ways you could've done better on the task. List that person's thoughts.

_____

_____

_____

The next time you do the task, note your starting time as before. As you do it, think about SLOWing yourself down and working on the areas you can improve on from your discussion. When you're done, note your finishing time.

Starting time: _____ Finishing time: _____ How long it took: _____

Rate the quality of your performance on the task using a scale of 1 to 10 (1 = poor; 10 = great). Circle your rating.

1   2   3   4   5   6   7   8   9   10

Now, have your parent or teacher rate the quality of your performance on the task using the same scale. Circle your parent or teacher's rating.

1   2   3   4   5   6   7   8   9   10

Did you take longer to do the task the second time? _____

What happened to both your and your parents or teacher's ratings? (Circle your answer.)

Improved   Stayed the same   Got worse

for you to know

Organizational skill is being able to keep things you need where they can be found quickly and easily so that you can be more efficient in your daily work. Being organized at school will help you get better grades; being organized at home will help make frustration (both yours and your parents') over not being able to find missing items less common. Being aware of how disorganization affects your life is the first step in improving this skill.

"Bryce, it's time to head to school!" Bryce's dad called to him from downstairs.

Bryce, seventeen, started scrambling. He grabbed his backpack, put on his shoes, and raced down the stairs, then doubled back because he had forgotten the paper he had been working on for his English class. He stuffed the paper into his backpack, snatched his jacket off the floor as he headed out the door, and hopped on the bus just as it arrived at his stop.

"Whew, I made it," he said as he sat down. Then he remembered that he had left his lunch at home on the counter. "Dang!" he said. He pulled out his cell phone and dialed his mom. "Could you bring my lunch to school for me?"

Bryce's mom sighed. "How many times do we have to go through this, Bryce? One day you forget your lunch; the next it's a book you need. You need to be more organized!"

In math class, Mr. Stangl told the students to get out their assignment from the day before. Bryce dug through his backpack and all his folders. When Mr. Stangl stopped at his desk, Bryce said, "I'm sure I finished it. I think I just left it at home. I promise to bring it in tomorrow."

Mr. Stangl said, "Well, Bryce, turning the assignment in tomorrow is okay, but you will have a lower grade because it is now late." Bryce made a mental note to put the math assignment in his backpack when he got home.

In chemistry class, Mr. Thompson told the students to get out a pencil for the test.

"Oh, no!" exclaimed Bryce. "I didn't know we had a test today!"

His lab partner reminded him, "Yeah, he told us about it yesterday."

Bryce sighed and took out a pencil. He didn't know most of the answers to the test because he hadn't spent any time studying. Oh well, maybe Mr. Thompson will let me retake the test after I've studied more, he thought.

When Bryce got home from school, he dropped his backpack on the floor in the kitchen, took off his shoes, grabbed a snack from the refrigerator, and plopped himself down in front of the TV. He watched an hour of television and then played some video games. After dinner, his mom asked him whether he had any homework.

"No, I did it all at school."

The next day, this process started all over again.

for you to do

See whether you can spot Bryce's disorganized behaviors. In the following chart, list the things that Bryce did or didn't do that made his day more hectic. Then write down the negative things that happened because of his disorganization. The first one has been done for you, as an example.

Disorganized Behavior Bryce Chose in the Story	How This Behavior Hurt Bryce (could be more than one consequence)
Not having homework in his backpack	• Having to scramble to catch the bus • Lower grades

more to do

Fill in the following chart with examples from your own life. Sometimes at first it isn't obvious how your disorganized behaviors can negatively affect you. So, think hard about all the areas of your life.

Disorganized Behavior in My Life	How This Behavior Hurts Me
Example: **messy backpack**	I can't find my homework assignments, so I get lower grades.

for you to know

A huge part of being organized is going through your belongings periodically and cleaning out unwanted or unneeded items. If you kept everything you ever received, you'd soon find yourself drowning in a sea of stuff! Getting rid of things you don't need on a weekly basis will allow you to be better organized and help you be able to find the things you need when you need them.

Tatiana, thirteen, kept her room a total mess, like many other girls her age. There were papers all over her desk, and there were clothes all over her floor. On her shelves there were half-finished bottles of water and candy wrappers. Tatiana didn't mind the mess. She swore that she could find anything she needed and therefore didn't have to clean her room.

Tatiana's backpack was in pretty much the same state. There were papers jammed into it from every angle. She could never find the papers she needed because they were all just crammed into any folder she could find. Because of this, her grades were suffering.

Each day, Tatiana's mom pleaded with her to clean her room and backpack. Tatiana would go into her room to clean it, but then she'd get distracted by something she found or a friend would call her. So, her room and backpack never seemed to get organized.

for you to do

Pick one area of your personal space that needs to be organized, and follow these easy steps to make a clean sweep:

1. Completely clean out or off the area to be organized. (You'll put the items that you want to keep back soon, but it helps to start with a clean slate.)

2. Sort all the items into three piles: one for those you want to keep, one for those you can discard, and one for those you can donate.

3. Choose an organizational system. For example, use different-colored folders for different classes, or put baskets on shelves to hold similar items.

4. Determine where the items you want to keep should go. For example, finished work should go on one side of a folder and unfinished work should go on the other, or all your video games should go in the same basket on the shelf.

5. Put away those items you want to keep according to your system, and get rid of the others. As a general rule, if you haven't used it in 6 months, you should probably get rid of it.

6. After a week, make sure the area is still organized. Repeat steps 1–4 if necessary.

7. Once you can keep this area successfully organized by spending a little time each week, do the same in another area. Start with the areas that are most important in your everyday life.

Try this method for several weeks at least. If, after this time, you find that it doesn't work for you, discuss with your parents another way to keep organized. Just be sure that the method you choose is easy to remember and use.

more to do

Make a copy of the following chart. Using this chart and the method of organizing just described, keep track of the areas of your life that need to be organized on a regular basis. For the first month, pick just one or two important areas (or write your own). When you've organized an area, place a check mark in the box for the week. Try adding an area each month as you get better at organizing your life.

Month: _____				
Area to Be Organized	Week 1	Week 2	Week 3	Week 4
Backpack				
Bedroom				
Binder				
Desk				
Locker				

Write about how you felt after organizing the area(s) above.

_____

What changes might you make next month?

_____

7 organizational tools

for you to know

In this age of technology, there are many different tools to help people stay organized. Experiment and discover which ones works best for you. The important thing is to find a tool that will allow you to keep track of all your responsibilities in one easy place.

Carlos, sixteen, had a terrible time keeping track of his assignments, his chores, his work schedule, and events that he needed to attend. Finally, after arriving late again to work one day, he decided that he had to find a way to get more organized. He sat down with his dad that evening, and together they discussed several options.

For the next several weeks, Carlos tried using the planner his school had provided to him at the beginning of the school year. It worked for a while, but he still seemed to forget important things because he'd forget to open the planner and check what was needed, or he forgot to write the events in his planner.

Carlos's parents then purchased an electronic organizer for him. They sat down with him and showed him how to enter all his appointments, homework assignments, projects, and chores. Then they set reminders that would go off at designated times before these tasks were due. Carlos began putting his tasks in the electronic organizer. Soon, he carried it with him everywhere. He loved that there was an alarm he could set, because the beep reminded him to look at the organizer to see what he had to do. Within a few days, he was doing much better at remembering his assignments and other tasks.

for you to do

Following is a list of tools that people commonly use to help them organize. Place a check mark next to any you currently use.

☐ **A paper calendar** is handy for a quick look at long-range planning.

☐ **An electronic calendar** is useful for reminders that things need to be done.

☐ **A cell phone (with calendar function)** will buzz or beep to remind you of calendar events you have entered.

☐ **Sticky notes** are good to jot reminders on to stick on a calendar or planner.

☐ **A backpack** is useful to keep all your school/work-related items in an easy-to-grab place.

☐ **A landing spot/takeoff pad** is the name for a spot near the door where you keep things you need when leaving the house.

☐ **Hooks** are useful for hanging backpacks, jackets, or keys so they can be found easily.

☐ **A desk organizer** is a good place to keep items like stapler, paper clips, and scissors.

☐ **Baskets** are useful for storing small items.

☐ **Bookcases** are a good place to put things you want to display (for example, trophies) and baskets containing small items, as well as books.

☐ **Desk trays** are helpful to keep papers you want to find quickly.

☐ **A filing cabinet** is useful for keeping papers and other documents that you don't want to throw away out of sight.

☐ **To-do lists** are helpful for jotting down what you need to accomplish each day.

☐ **An over-the-door shoe organizer** is good for small, easily lost items you need to find quickly (not just shoes).

☐ **An accordion file** is a useful organization system for carrying with you in a backpack.

Now, pick one or two tools from the list that you'd like to add to those you're already using. How can you use them to help you stay organized?

_____

_____

_____

Your parent will probably be glad to help you obtain these tools (if necessary) if you explain that you're trying to get more organized. Try using these tools on a regular basis for a week or two and see what happens.

more to do

After trying a couple of new tools from the previous exercise, answer the following questions.

Which of these tools seemed to work best for you and why?

_____

_____

_____

_____

Which didn't work so well for you and why?

_____

_____

_____

_____

Keep trying different tools until you find several that best help you keep your life organized. Be sure to practice using each tool every day for at least a week—give it a chance to work—before moving on to a new tool. Also, think about ways to put the tools you currently have to new uses. For example, a shoe organizer can organize shoes, but you can also use it as a study tool: Put a flash card and a piece of candy in each slot. Quiz yourself using the cards; if you get the answer to the question correct, you get the candy. Organization and motivation in one easy place!

8 how do you use your time?

for you to know

Time management ability is the ability to understand how to use your time to your advantage. Too often, you may find yourself surfing the Internet, playing video games, or watching television rather than working on what you need to accomplish. As you get older and more mature, you'll realize that sometimes doing the things you *have to* do will give you more time for the things you *want to* do.

In the morning, fourteen-year-old Beth got up, ate breakfast, and began getting ready for school. As she was packing to leave, she received a text from her friend Ashley. Because Beth decided to text Ashley back, she ended up running late and missed the bus. Since she had to wait for her mom to finish getting ready for work before she could get a ride, Beth was late for school and had to stop by the office to get a pass.

On the way home from school, Beth stopped by her friend Tami's house to play some video games. At six o'clock, Beth's mom called her for dinner and she went home.

After dinner, Beth turned on the TV and saw that her favorite show was on. She watched two other shows after that. Finally, at ten o'clock, her mom asked her whether her homework was finished.

"Yeah, I think so."

As Beth was getting ready for bed, she remembered that she had a history test the next day. Now she was faced with a tough decision: stay up late to study, or go to bed? She decided that she was too tired to study and would take her chances on the test.

...Unfortunately, Beth didn't pass the history test.

You can probably tell that Beth needs to manage her time better when she's not in school.

for you to do

Place a check mark next to any of the following activities you engage in often. "Time wasters" are those activities that suck up time and don't help you do what needs to be done. "Time users" are those activities that get things done. Use the blanks to add other activities you do that fit the category.

Time Wasters	Time Users
☐ Watching TV	☐ Completing homework
☐ Playing video games	☐ Practicing your instrument
☐ Texting	☐ Studying for a test
☐ Surfing the Internet	☐ Cleaning the house
☐ Talking on the phone	☐ Finishing a craft project
☐ _____	☐ _____
☐ _____	☐ _____
☐ _____	☐ _____

If there are more check marks in the first column than the second, you're probably spending too much time on things that are less likely to help you be successful in life or school.

Note that many activities, including the ones listed above, can be *either* "time wasters" or "time users," depending on how you use them. If you're using an activity to avoid a task you should be doing—for example, if you're cleaning the house as an excuse to put off making a dreaded but necessary phone call—then it would probably be considered a "time waster." If, however, an activity like surfing the Internet or watching TV is part of an assignment, then it would probably be considered a "time user."

more to do

Prioritizing is determining (1) which activities are most important and need your immediate attention and (2) which activities are less important, but still need to be done.

Look at the following list of activities from Beth's day. Help her prioritize them by putting a 1 next to those activities of high importance, a 2 next to those of medium importance, and a 3 next to those of low importance. Then make a list of the different activities *you* have to do during a typical day and prioritize them in the same way you did Beth's. Finally, answer the questions at the end.

Beth's Activities

_____ Study for test.   _____ Text Ashley.

_____ Get ready for school.   _____ Eat dinner.

_____ Play video games.   _____ Catch the bus.

_____ Eat breakfast.   _____ Go to bed on time.

_____ Stop in office to get pass.

My Activities

_____   _____

_____   _____

_____   _____

_____   _____

Which of your activities did you assign a 1 to? _____

_____

Why did you rate these activities as highly important?

_____

Which of your activities did you assign a 2 to? _____

_____

Why did you rate these activities as moderately important?

_____

Which of your activities did you assign a 3 to? _____

_____

Why did you rate these activities as not very important?

_____

List some of the reasons that might make one activity more important than another activity.

_____

_____

_____

_____

_____

9 scheduling your time

for you to know

Teens with weakness in executive functioning can't always plan out when, how, and where they should do things. For these reasons, a schedule can be a very important tool. Being able to see at a glance what's coming up can be very helpful and lessen your stress.

When Arianne was younger, her mom scheduled all her appointments, playdates, and sports practices and matches. Now that she was thirteen, her mom expected her to begin doing these things on her own. Her mom even purchased a huge wall calendar for her to keep track of her activities. Arianne wasn't sure where to start. Since her friend Tina was really good at organizing and scheduling her time, Arianne asked Tina to come over to help her fill out her calendar.

Tina told Arianne that the first step was to write in the most important activities; those that she had to do on a specific date and time. After Arianne entered those, Tina told her that she should write in all the things that she had to accomplish not necessarily on a specific date and time. Only then could Arianne write in those things she wanted to do, fitting them in around the activities already on the calendar. Then Arianne's month would be all planned out. All she'd need to do was add in anything that came up at the last minute, making sure it fit in somewhere.

for you to do

Following is Arianne's calendar, with the activities she has to do at specific times already on it. Help Arianne fill in the rest of her calendar with (listed after the calendar) the things she has to do that are more flexible and the things she wants to do.

September						
Sunday	Monday	Tuesday	Wednesday	Thursday	Friday	Saturday
	1	2 Soccer Practice 6:00–8:00 p.m.	3	4	5	6 Soccer Game 12:00–2:00 p.m.
7 Church 8:00–9:00 a.m.	8	9 Soccer Practice 6:00–8:00 p.m.	10	11	12 Mom's Birthday Dinner 7:00–9:00 p.m.	13 Soccer Game 12:00–2:00 p.m.
14 Church 8:00–9:00 a.m.	15 Dentist 4:00 p.m.	16 Soccer Practice 6:00–8:00 p.m.	17	18	19	20 Soccer Game 12:00–2:00 p.m.
21 Church 8:00–9:00 a.m.	22 Speech in English	23 Soccer Practice 6:00–8:00 p.m.	24	25 Science Test	26	27 Soccer Game 12:00–2:00 p.m.
28 Church 8:00–9:00 a.m.	29	30 Soccer Practice 6:00–8:00 p.m.				

Clean Bedroom (once a week)

Walk Dog (every night)

Watch Favorite Show (Thursdays 6:00–7:00 p.m.)

Study for Science Test (two nights a week from the ninth through the twenty-fourth)

Go to Movie with Tina (any open Saturday)

Prepare for Speech (two nights a week from the ninth through the twenty-first)

more to do

Now it's your turn. Make a copy of the following calendar template. After labeling it with month and dates, write in all the things you need to do and then those you want to do. This will be a visual reminder of what needs to be done when. Do this for every month, or purchase a wall calendar.

Sunday	Monday	Tuesday	Wednesday	Thursday	Friday	Saturday

10 daily planning

for you to know

While a calendar is important for long-range planning, you may find that it helps to have a daily planner as well. A *daily planner* is simply a way to keep track of the tasks you need to do each day. Planners come in many different styles. A planner may take the form of a printed notebook, an electronic device, or software for your computer, smart phone, or tablet. Find the one that works best for you, and use it on a regular basis.

Raven, an eighth-grader, had been working on her executive skills for several weeks. Mrs. Thrasher, her school counselor, had been giving her weekly assignments that taught her to organize her life, start setting long-term goals, and complete her schoolwork and homework on a regular basis. Now, Mrs. Thrasher believed that Raven was ready to start planning her tasks on her own. She explained to Raven the importance of using a daily planner of some kind. She showed her how to write assignments, appointments, and chores in a planner and to check them off when they were done. For the next week, Raven practiced using a planner, and Mrs. Thrasher checked each day to see how she was doing with it. On Friday, Mrs. Thrasher gave Raven a reward for filling out her planner correctly all week and for completing all the tasks she had entered.

After several weeks of practice, Raven became an expert at filling out and using her planner on a daily basis to stay on track.

for you to do

Here's some practice with a basic planner format.

In the following chart, list up to ten tasks you need to do tomorrow between the time you get up and the time you go to bed, in the order in which they need to be done. Write the time frame for each one as well. Tomorrow, after you complete a task, place a check mark in the "Done" column.

Done	Task	Time
✓	Example: **Wake up**	*6:00* a.m.

more to do

Using a planner can be a big help, but you still can't get a task done if you don't have the required materials. For example, you can't study for a history test if you don't have your history notes or your history book.

Choose one of the tasks you listed in the previous exercise and answer the following questions to be sure you have all the required materials next time.

Task to be completed: _____

When does this task need to be completed by? _____

What items do I need to complete this task?

_____

_____

Where can I get these items?

_____

_____

Who might be able to help me with completing this task? _____

for you to know

Feelings are emotional energy, and handling them appropriately is a huge part of becoming an adult. Teens who have trouble with tasks that require executive skills have not yet developed the ability to handle the strong emotions that can arise in certain situations. Knowing where your feelings come from is a huge first step in learning to control them.

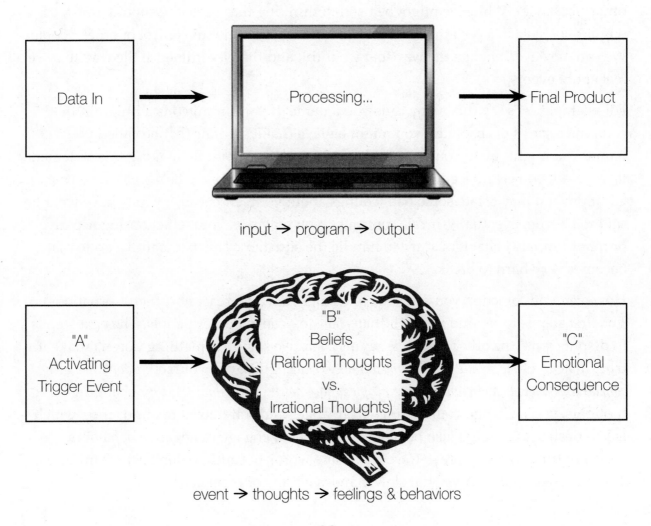

| Data In | → | Processing... | → | Final Product |

input → program → output

| "A" Activating Trigger Event | → | "B" Beliefs (Rational Thoughts vs. Irrational Thoughts) | → | "C" Emotional Consequence |

event → thoughts → feelings & behaviors

Our brains are like computers. Computer output (what's displayed on the screen, for example) is based not only on input (what we type in, for example), but also on what type of program is running. The rules for what to do with the input are contained in the program. In much the same way, our feelings and behaviors are based not only on the events in our lives, but also on the way we think about them. When we "run" negative (irrational) thoughts about the events in our lives, the output is negative feelings and behaviors. When we run positive (rational) thoughts about the events in our lives, the output is positive feelings and behaviors.

Many times our brains operate according to a series of rules—statements that contain "shoulds," "musts," "ought tos," and other *absolutes*. Often these rules are regarding others' behavior. While we might be used to thinking that someone should, must, or ought to behave in a certain way, the truth is that we are not in control of other people. We can, however, change the way that we think and thereby influence the way that we feel about events.

For example, let's say that a boy calls you a name. If your brain runs a program that contains a series of absolutes, you might believe that it's unfair that he called you a name. You might say to yourself, *He should not call me a name*. By making this statement to yourself, you create feelings of anger toward the boy because he's breaking a rule. In addition, you may create some bad feelings about yourself because you believe what he said to be true. Eventually, if this continues, you may find yourself choosing negative or inappropriate behaviors to try to handle the situation. This turns into a cycle that becomes very hard to break.

However, with practice, you can start to change how you react in difficult situations. The first step is to remind yourself that you can't control other people. The next step is to dispute what the other person is saying, because saying something doesn't make it true. Instead of *He should not call me a name*, you might say to yourself, *I don't like being called names, but I can't control other people, and what he said is not true*. By changing your thoughts, you'll change your feelings from anger and self-hatred to annoyance, which is less destructive. You'll also be much less likely to engage in negative behaviors, which in turn will help break the cycle. Some words of caution: don't expect miracles. These changes will happen, but slowly and with lots of practice.

for you to do

Read the following chart one row at a time, imagining what you'd do or how you'd feel if the event in the first column happened and you had the thought in the second column. Write your answer in the third column. The first one has been done for you, as an example.

Event	Irrational Belief	Feeling or Behavior
Someone calls you a name.	He *should* not do that.	Example: **hit the person who called me a name**
Your parents yell at you.	That's *unfair.*	
Your boyfriend or girlfriend breaks up with you.	I'm *not lovable.*	
You spill your milk.	I'm such a *klutz.*	
You get an F on a test.	I *should* have gotten a better grade.	
Event	Rational Belief	
Someone calls you a name.	Wow, he's got a problem.	
Your parents yell at you.	Sometimes I get on my parents' nerves.	
Your boyfriend or girlfriend breaks up with you.	I'm still a lovable person.	
You spill your milk.	That's unfortunate.	
You get an F on a test.	I'll need to study more for the next test.	

Look back over your responses. Were the feelings you imagined having and the things you imagined yourself doing in response to each event more positive, or at least less negative, when the belief was rational?

more to do

Think of all the feelings you can remember having during the past week. List them; then, for each one, note the situation that you believe caused that feeling.

Feeling   **Situation**

1. _____

2. _____

3. _____

4. _____

5. _____

List the thoughts you remember having during each of these situations.

1. _____

2. _____

3. _____

4. _____

5. _____

Identify the absolutes in your thoughts (the "musts" or "shoulds"). List them.

_____

_____

Choose one of your thoughts that contains an absolute, and rephrase it using gentler, more forgiving words.

_____

_____

Does this help you feel differently about the situation? _____

Practice rephrasing the remaining statements using gentler, more forgiving words, and see how your feelings might be different if you encounter these situations in the future.

12 understanding your feelings

for you to know

Feelings are emotional energy. They're an indication that something in your life needs to either continue or change, depending on the emotion you're experiencing. Feelings themselves are neither good nor bad, but what you do with them can be good or bad. In order to manage your feelings, you need to understand them at their deepest level.

Jacob, an eighth-grader, had just gotten out of Mr. Bright's language arts class late because the other students wouldn't follow Mr. Bright's direction to quiet down, so he made the whole class stay after the bell. Jacob was walking quickly to get to Mrs. Delaney's math class on time when Scott, another eighth-grade student, ran smack into him, knocking his books and papers all over the floor. Scott didn't bother to apologize or even acknowledge that he had bumped into Jacob. As Scott continued on his way, Jacob started screaming at him.

"Stop and pick up my books, you idiot!"

Scott paid no attention and kept walking. By the time he had picked up all his books and papers, Jacob no longer had a chance of beating the bell. He got to Mrs. Delaney's class two minutes late.

"Please give me your behavior card, Jacob," Mrs. Delaney said when he walked in.

"But someone knocked my books on the floor, Mrs. D.—that's why I'm late."

"No arguments, Jacob. I need your behavior card, please."

Jacob dug out his card and gave it to Mrs. Delaney, who punched one of the small Xs in the corner.

By this time, Jacob was so angry about what had happened that he couldn't even pay attention in math. Afterward, as he headed to lunch, he fumed about how unfair it was that Mrs. Delaney had given him a punch on his card for something that wasn't even his fault. When he got to the lunch line, he saw Scott laughing and joking around with a friend. Jacob walked right up to Scott and pushed him, hard.

Scott whirled around and asked, "What was that for, jerk?"

"For being an idiot!" Jacob spat.

Soon, both boys were pushing and shoving. Mr. Bright stepped in and escorted them to the office to wait for the principal.

for you to do

Circle all the words you think describe how Jacob felt over the course of the preceding story.

Happy	Frustrated	Embarrassed	Inferior
Sad	Scared	Annoyed	Delighted
Angry	Worried	Unsure	Rejected
Disappointed	Excited	Shy	

How many did you circle? _____

Do you think it's possible to experience more than one feeling at once? Why or why not?

_____

_____

_____

What event(s) in the story do you believe "triggered" Jacob to react the way he did?

_____

_____

_____

What do you imagine Jacob said to himself before, during, and/or after each event in the story?

_____

_____

_____

_____

List one or two things Jacob could've done differently for each event in the story.

_____

_____

_____

_____

more to do

In the following box, use colored pencils or markers to write the names of all the feelings you've experienced recently. Write each feeling in the color, size, and shape you believe best represent it. Next to each feeling, write whatever message you think the feeling is trying to send you. For example, if you wrote FRUSTRATION, the message might be that you need to ask for help with whatever's frustrating you. If you wrote HAPPY, the message might be that things are going well in some area of your life at present. Then, circle those messages that indicate something in your life needs to change. Think about ways you can change what needs to be changed. If you can't change them by yourself, ask for help.

13 handling your negative feelings

for you to know

No matter how hard you try, or how often you practice replacing them with positive feelings, there will be times when it's next to impossible to stop your negative feelings. They may show up when your parents criticize you for not getting your chores done or when your teacher tells you for the umpteenth time that you need to work harder to get your assignments in on time. Keep in mind, we all experience negative emotions from time to time, so knowing what to do when they come is a good skill to learn.

Studies have shown that if athletes visualize themselves winning an important game before they play, they're actually more likely to win, because they've already seen the positive outcome. In *mental imagery*, we use the power of the mind to help us create what we'd like to have happen. It works for just about any situation. If you want to get better grades, visualize yourself successfully completing the work before you attempt it. While you'll still need to do the work, you may find yourself more motivated. In addition, visualization can help you create positive feelings about yourself and your situation.

for you to do

Circle all the negative feelings you've experienced within the past two weeks.

Ashamed	Bossed around	Unloved
Disrespected	Pressured	Blamed
Embarrassed	Alone	Judged
Insulted	Confused	Afraid
Put down	Discouraged	Scared
Teased	Ignored	Threatened
Worthless	Rejected	Untrusted

Choose one of the feelings you circled, and write about the situation surrounding it.

_____

_____

_____

_____

What could you have done differently in that situation that might have created a better outcome?

_____

_____

_____

_____

Rewrite your description of the situation as if you had in fact responded in this different way.

_____

_____

_____

_____

Read the situation as you rewrote it several times. Then, close your eyes and play this scene in your head. That is, vividly and in as much detail as you can, imagine doing what you said you could've done differently in the situation.

Write down any differences in your feelings between the real situation and the imagined situation. What do you think are the reasons for these differences?

_____

_____

more to do

When we experience negative emotions, our bodies become tense.

In order to combat bodily tension due to negative emotions, try the following progressive relaxation exercise. It may work best if you do it while listening to some relaxing music.

1. Sit down, or lie down in a comfortable position. Loosen any tight clothing. Close your eyes. Just try to relax and let go of all your thoughts and stress.

2. Take in a deep breath, hold it for a beat, and let it out. Repeat two times. With each breath, feel your body relaxing more and more.

3. Tense your lower legs. Tighten your calves, your ankles, your feet, and your toes. Pretend that you're pulling your toes apart as you tense all the muscles in your lower legs. Hold this tension as you breathe in deeply, and hold that breath for a beat. As you let out your breath, let go of all the tension in your lower legs. Repeat.

4. Tense your thighs and buttocks. Hold this tension as you breathe in deeply, and hold that breath for a beat. As you let out your breath, let go of all the tension in your thighs and buttocks. Repeat.

5. Tense your abdomen and chest. Hold this tension as you breathe in deeply, and hold that breath for a beat. As you let out your breath, let go of all the tension in your abdomen and chest. Repeat.

6. Make your hands into fists and tense all the muscles in your shoulders, arms, wrists, and fingers. Hold this tension as you breathe in deeply, and hold that breath for a beat. As you let out your breath, let go of all the tension in your shoulders, arms, wrists, and fingers. Repeat.

7. Tense your neck, head, and face. Hold this tension as you breathe in deeply, and hold that breath for a beat. As you let out your breath, let go of all the tension in your neck, head, and face. Repeat.

8. Quietly scan your body for any remaining tension. If you find tension, concentrate on letting it go from your body. Take another three deep breaths and let them out. When you get up, you will feel completely relaxed. You will feel stress-free and content. Go to sleep, or go about your day and feel completely calm and worry-free.

Practice this method of relaxation whenever you experience negative emotions. If you can't do it immediately after having a negative emotion, then do it before you go to bed each day. After a while, you should notice that you're having fewer problems with negative emotions.

what's an impulse? 14

for you to know

An *impulse* is an immediate desire to move your body or take action. People who obey their impulses without thinking about the possible consequences are often described as "impulsive." If you're impulsive, you typically act first, then question later whether the action was a good one. Many times, teens who act impulsively can get into trouble with parents, teachers, or the law.

Chiara, a sixth-grader, was forever interrupting adults. Her reasoning was that if she didn't say what was on her mind, she might forget. Chiara also blurted out answers in class. Before the teacher could even finish her thought, Chiara would have the answer. Similarly, she often started assignments before reading all the directions, with the result that sometimes she didn't do what she was supposed to, and her grades suffered for it.

Several times, Chiara got into trouble with her parents and teachers over bad decisions that she knew better than to make. For instance, she'd go to a friend's house after school without letting her parents know, or she'd copy answers from other students in class. Once, she took a bracelet she liked from the store without paying for it. Her friends found it hard to be with her because they didn't want to get in trouble too when she did things like that—when she acted impulsively.

53

for you to do

Imagine that the following outline represents your body. Put an X on the areas of the body in which you feel the urge to move or act.

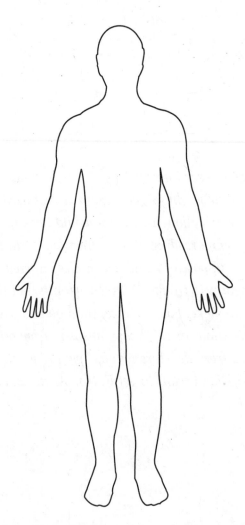

Write down the types of things you do that are impulsive (done without thinking of the consequences).

_____

_____

more to do

Many times, impulsive teens are told to stop doing the impulsive behavior; however, it's not that simple. It takes time to turn an old habit around. Still, remembering to STOP can help you make better choices more often. STOP stands for Stop, Think, Observe, and Plan.

S—Stop what you're doing.

T—Think about why you did what you just did.

O—Observe how what you just did affected the people involved.

P—Plan what to do differently next time.

Try it now. Choose one of the impulsive acts you wrote down in the previous exercise, and imagine that you just did it. Answer the following questions, which use the STOP format, to help you think of a better action—maybe one that would get you a little of what you desire now, or one that would help you get it later, without the negative consequences.

Stop what you're doing.

What did you just do (the impulsive act)? _____

Think about why you did what you just did.

Why did you just do that? (Place a check mark next to all that apply.)

☐ To avoid an adult   ☐ To get adult attention   ☐ To get items/
                                                        activities

☐ To avoid a peer   ☐ To get peer attention

                                                    ☐ I don't know
☐ To avoid a task

Observe how what you just did affected the people involved.

How were the people involved affected? _____

_____

Plan what to do differently next time.

Write what you'll try instead to get what you want in the future.

_____

_____

_____

_____

_____

_____

look before you leap 15

---

for you to know

A *consequence* is what happens as a result of choosing to act or not to act in any given situation. Sometimes consequences can be positive; sometimes they can be negative. Many times, teens who struggle with impulsivity experience only the negative consequences of their actions.

Sometimes it can be hard for teens with weakness in executive functioning to think about the consequences of an action *before* they do it. It seems as if they can't stop themselves from doing things that they know might turn out badly for them. Examining the possible consequences of your actions can be a valuable skill to learn. If you practice thinking quickly about what might happen *before* you choose an action, hopefully you'll become better at making positive decisions for yourself.

for you to do

Making good decisions is all about looking at what might happen if you were to do something *before* you actually do it.

Following are several actions you might take. For each action, try to think of one positive and one negative likely consequence, and write them in the blanks. It may be hard to think of a positive consequence for something that seems bad (or a negative consequence for something that seems good), but if you really try, you can probably come up with something. For example, if you won tickets to a concert, the positive consequence might be that you get to enjoy a night out at no charge. However, the negative consequence might be that you have to miss a favorite TV show.

Action: You purchase a lottery ticket.

　　Positive consequence: _____

　　Negative consequence: _____

Action: You eat doughnuts for breakfast.

　　Positive consequence: _____

　　Negative consequence: _____

Action: You do your chores.

　　Positive consequence: _____

　　Negative consequence: _____

Action: You don't complete your homework.

　　Positive consequence: _____

　　Negative consequence: _____

Action: You talk to your friends on the phone.

Positive consequence: _____

Negative consequence: _____

Action: You yell something out in class.

Positive consequence: _____

Negative consequence: _____

Action: You talk back to your parents.

Positive consequence: _____

Negative consequence: _____

Action: You interrupt a conversation.

Positive consequence: _____

Negative consequence: _____

more to do

Sometimes the results of our actions are not immediately apparent. We may have to wait days, months, or even years to see how a decision will turn out. When the consequences are not immediate, it can be harder to make good decisions. For example, because smoking-related health problems take years to develop, a young person who smokes may not experience any immediate negative consequences and therefore think that it's okay.

Think of some immediate and long-term consequences for the following decisions.

Decision: Eat junk food.

   Immediate consequences: _____

   Long-term consequences: _____

Decision: Drink alcohol.

   Immediate consequences: _____

   Long-term consequences: _____

Decision: Exercise.

   Immediate consequences: _____

   Long-term consequences: _____

Decision: Complete my homework.

   Immediate consequences: _____

   Long-term consequences: _____

Now write some decisions you've recently made that might have long-term consequences, and do the same for them.

Decision: _____

    Immediate consequences: _____

    Long-term consequences: _____

Decision: _____

    Immediate consequences: _____

    Long-term consequences: _____

Decision: _____

    Immediate consequences: _____

    Long-term consequences: _____

Decision: _____

    Immediate consequences: _____

    Long-term consequences: _____

Decision: _____

    Immediate consequences: _____

    Long-term consequences: _____

16 standing up to your peers

for you to know

Peer pressure is one of those things that all teens have to learn how to deal with. However, for teens with weakness in the area of behavior control, this rite of passage can be fraught with hazards. Teens who don't control their behavior are more likely to go along with what their peers tell them to do, which may not always be in their best interest.

Omar, sixteen, had many friends. He liked to hang out with them on the weekends. One Saturday, his friend Bill asked him to smoke a cigarette. Omar didn't want to look like "a baby" to his friends, so he accepted the cigarette from Bill.

Tracy and her friend Sue, both seventeen, were shopping in a clothing store. Sue told Tracy to go into the changing room and put on a pair of jeans under her sweats. When Tracy objected, Sue said, "Come on—everyone takes things once in a while. Who will it hurt?"

Franklin, fourteen, asked John whether he could copy his homework. John said that he didn't think it was a good idea, but Franklin pressed him, arguing that no one would find out.

for you to do

In each of the following pictures, someone is being pressured to do something that might get him or her into trouble. Under each picture, write how the person being pressured could say no to the other person.

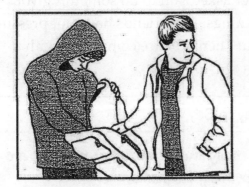

_____

_____

_____

_____

_____

_____

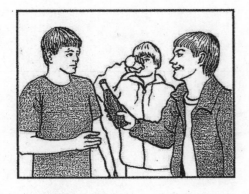

_____

_____

_____

_____

_____

_____

more to do

Even if you've never felt pressured to do the things pictured in the previous exercise, it's a good idea to learn how you can say no to your friends politely and still feel good about yourself.

Think about whether any of your friends has ever asked you to do something you didn't want to. In the following chart, list some things your friends have put pressure on you to do that you knew weren't right for you. Then practice coming up with a reason not to do each one.

Behavior Friend Asked You to Do	Way to Say No
Example: **play video games instead of doing homework.**	**I'd really like to, but my parents are expecting me home.**

flexibility 17

for you to know

Being flexible is an important skill to learn. Flexible people are much better at handling unplanned situations. But teens with weakness in executive functioning often find it hard to be flexible.

A popular toy of years past was called Stretch Armstrong. Stretch Armstrong was an oversized action figure that could be pulled, bent, or shaped in many different ways. Kids could even tie Stretch's arms and legs together. This ability to bend, mold, stretch, or shape something is flexibility. Physical flexibility is important to athletes, who put their bodies through a wide range of motion. And people who exercise often warm up by stretching, to prevent tearing a muscle. However, physical flexibility is only one area of flexibility. Other areas include emotional flexibility and mental flexibility. Teens who are not very emotionally or mentally flexible have a hard time moving from task to task, as well as difficulty handling unplanned changes to their schedule.

Just as you can improve your physical flexibility, so too can you improve your emotional and mental flexibility through exercise and practice.

for you to do

Follow the directions for each part of the exercise. You'll need six colored pencils, markers, or crayons: green, yellow, orange, blue, red, and purple.

1. Color each shape the color listed below it.

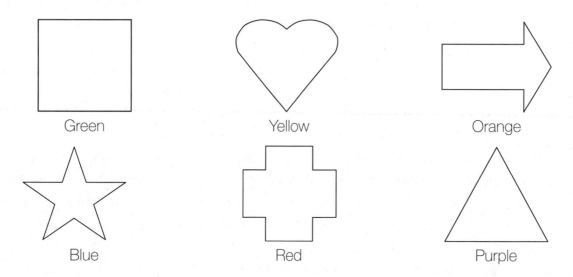

Green	Yellow	Orange
Blue	Red	Purple

2. Do *not* color any of these words.

Green	**Yellow**	**Orange**
Blue	**Red**	**Purple**

3. Color each of the following words a color *different* from the color named. For example, color the word "green" any color *but* green.

Green	**Yellow**	**Orange**
Blue	**Red**	**Purple**

more to do

Using a watch with a second hand, or a stopwatch, record how long it takes you to name all the colors of the shapes in part 1 of the previous exercise.

_____ seconds

Then, record how long it takes you to read the words listed in part 2 (which you didn't color).

_____ seconds

Finally, record how long it takes you to name all the colors of the words (the colors you used, not what the words say) in part 3, one by one (repeating if necessary).

_____ seconds

Practice naming the colors in part 3 for one minute, then time yourself again.

_____ seconds

Did your time decrease? (Circle your answer.)

    Yes   No

Why do you think this is?

_____

What does this activity help you understand about your mental flexibility?

_____

_____

_____

18 improvising

---

for you to know

Teens who struggle with tasks that require executive skills tend to be less mentally flexible than their peers. One way to increase your mental flexibility is to practice *improvising*. Improvising is when you come up with a creative solution to a problem using whatever tools and materials you have on hand, even if they aren't strictly speaking the best ones for the job. Improvising often requires imagination, which is a powerful tool itself.

Sometimes when we improvise we come up with a story to fit the situation we find ourselves in. Actors who want to improve their acting skills study this kind of improvisation. When parents tell their children a bedtime story that they make up as they go along, that's also improvisation. Any time you came up with a solution to a problem "on the fly," you likely improvised a bit. Improvising, or being resourceful, can mean finding a new use for an object or making use of an object in a different way than usual—for example, using a pair of tongs rather than standing on a chair or stepstool to reach something on a high shelf in your kitchen.

for you to do

Write as many creative (that is, other than normal) uses for each of the following items as you can. The first one has been done for you, as an example.

Safety Pin

Normal use: to fasten cloth together

Creative uses: **to hold papers together, as an earring, to clean between your teeth, to remove a sliver, to open an envelope**

Fork

Normal use: to eat

Creative uses: _____

Pillow

Normal use: to rest your head

Creative uses: _____

Hammer

Normal use: to pound nails into wood

Creative uses: _____

Toothbrush

Normal use: to clean your teeth

Creative uses: _____

Bandage

Normal use: to cover a wound

Creative uses: _____

more to do

Many times in life, things you don't expect to happen will happen. When this occurs, it helps if you're ready to "go with the flow."

Write how you could improvise what you'd do in each of the following situations. The first one has been done for you, as an example.

Situation: You've planned a birthday party with enough food for six people, but ten people show up.

Example: **Think of a dish I can whip up quickly so that there will be enough food for everyone.**

Situation: You've planned to hang out with a friend at the mall, but your parent calls to tell you that your grandparents are coming over for dinner and you need to come home.

_____

_____

Situation: In math class, your teacher announces a pop quiz. You haven't prepared for this possibility by studying at all.

_____

_____

Situation: You're feeding your dog and the top comes off the container. Food spills all over the floor, and your mom will be home soon.

_____

_____

Situation: While you're cleaning your room, a friend texts you asking you to go see a movie. You want to, but if you don't get your room clean, you'll be grounded.

_____

_____

Situation: You have to be at your new job in a half hour, but the clothes you need to wear are dirty.

_____

_____

Situation: You're working on a history project for school on the computer when suddenly the power goes out. You haven't saved your project.

_____

_____

19 perspective matters

for you to know

Your *perspective* is your way of looking at the world. Some people have an optimistic perspective; they "see the glass as half full." Others have a pessimistic perspective; they "see the glass as half empty." Fortunately, perspectives can change.

Greg, seventeen, had a chip on his shoulder. He assumed that his friends were only interested in hanging out with him because he could drive. He thought that his teachers hated him. He believed that his parents were out to make his life miserable. As a result, Greg was always angry. He woke up grumpy, he picked fights with friends, and he argued with his parents on a daily basis. Finally, Greg had had enough. He went to his school counselor to see whether there was something she could do to get people to stop bugging him.

His counselor explained that there was only one person Greg could control: himself. She said that his pessimism and expecting the worst from people affected the way he treated others and thus the way they treated him. At first, Greg didn't want to believe that. He spent a lot of time trying to get his counselor to see how everyone else was making him miserable. Finally, after several meetings, Greg started to think that maybe his counselor was right. Instead of looking for negatives all the time, he tried to find the positives. He started looking at his friends differently. Turns out, his friends weren't only interested in him because he could drive—they liked hanging out with him, and they let him drive because they thought that he wanted to. When he started to make an effort to get along with his parents and do his chores, his parents stopped arguing with him. His teachers were much happier when he began completing assignments. Because people treated him differently once he changed his perspective and behavior, Greg was happier too.

for you to do

Your perspective is like a pair of tinted glasses that colors the world you see. Seeing people and events in your life in a "negative" color can cause you to become a more negative person.

On the lines below the glasses, write two negative ways of looking at each of the following situations. You can write negative thoughts or negative predictions. Then ask yourself how you'd feel if you looked at the situation in this way. Write the name of a feeling, and circle the degree to which you think you would feel it on a scale of 1 to 5, where 1 is mild and 5 is intense.

Situation 1. You come home from school and your mom tells you that you need to do the dishes.

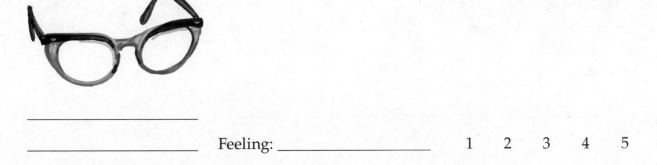

_____

_____   Feeling: _____   1   2   3   4   5

Situation 2. Your teacher assigns you a project that requires you to create a presentation and deliver it to the class.

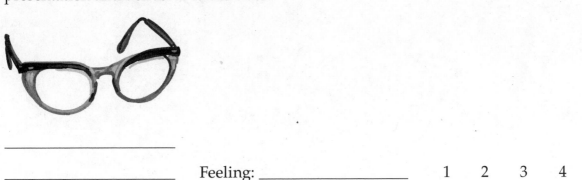

_____

_____   Feeling: _____   1   2   3   4   5

Situation 3. Your dentist tells you that you have a cavity.

_____

_____   Feeling: _____   1   2   3   4   5

Situation 4. You're let go from your job because of a slowdown in business.

_____

_____   Feeling: _____   1   2   3   4   5

more to do

For each of the situations in the previous exercise, shift your perspective and come up with two positive ways of looking at the situation. How would you feel if you looked at the situation in this way? Write the name of a feeling, and circle the degree to which you think you would feel it on a scale of 1 to 5, where 1 is mild and 5 is intense.

Situation 1. You come home from school and your mom tells you that you need to do the dishes.

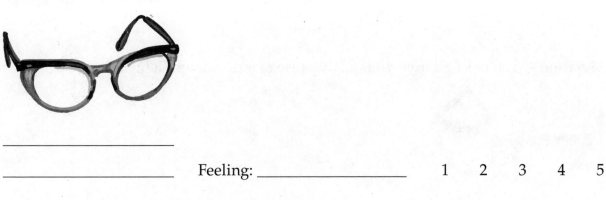

_____

_____   Feeling: _____   1   2   3   4   5

Situation 2. Your teacher assigns you a project that requires you to create a presentation and deliver it to the class.

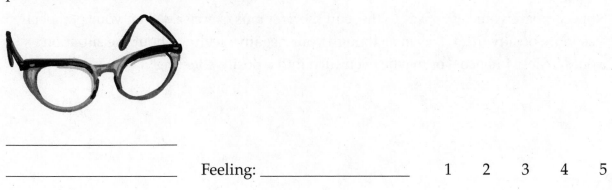

_____

_____   Feeling: _____   1   2   3   4   5

Situation 3. Your dentist tells you that you have a cavity.

_____

_____   Feeling: _____   1   2   3   4   5

Situation 4. You're let go from your job because of a slowdown in business.

_____

_____   Feeling: _____   1   2   3   4   5

Now compare your responses to those in the previous exercise. When your perspective was more positive, did it seem as though your negative feeling about the situation would be less intense—or maybe even turn into a positive feeling?

procrastination problems 20

for you to know

Procrastination is putting off a task that you'd rather not do. Many times when teens with weakness in executive functioning are faced with a boring task, they tell themselves that they'll get to it later and choose to do something fun in the meantime. Yet even if you temporarily distract yourself by doing something you'd rather do, waiting until later only increases your stress about doing the task and makes it less likely that you'll have time to do it properly or to the best of your ability.

Scott, fifteen, always seemed to have difficulty starting and completing tasks at home. His mom and dad would constantly remind him to "get going" on chores. He always seemed to find something else to do instead of what he needed to be doing.

At one family meeting, Scott's dad finally asked him about this procrastination. Scott replied that he didn't like doing chores or homework; he found them "boring." His parents listened and decided that he should use the timer on the stove to set a time limit for working on homework and chores. When the timer went off, he'd be finished for the day. Each week, he should decrease the amount of time on the timer by one minute.

At first, Scott couldn't complete the task before the timer went off. He noticed that many times wouldn't start right away when the timer was set. Because he noticed this, the next time he started the task immediately after he set the timer. Before long, Scott was consistently completing his chores and homework before the timer went off. Once he realized how much time he'd been wasting, he found that he could have more time to do the things he wanted to as soon as his chores and homework were done.

for you to do

Some teens procrastinate because they don't know how to start a task. Others procrastinate because they fear that they'll fail, they'll look foolish, or others will see them as incapable.

Think about the tasks you might procrastinate on, and list them in the first column. In the second column, write why you think you don't want to do each task.

Task Being Avoided	Reason for Avoiding It
Example: **putting away the dishes**	**I don't know where they're supposed to go.**

more to do

Many times, procrastination will cause problems in your life.

In the following frame, draw a picture that shows a time when you procrastinated on a task. Then answer the related questions.

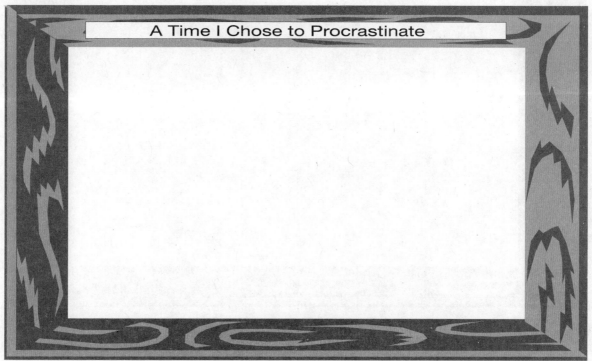

A Time I Chose to Procrastinate

What situation was this?

_____

Why did you avoid this task?

_____

What problems did this create for you?

_____

How did you feel? _____

In this next frame, draw a picture that shows a time when you did a task *without* procrastinating. Then answer the related questions.

What situation was this?

_____

Why did you choose not to avoid this task?

_____

What positive things happened because you completed this task?

_____

How did you feel? _____

Look at the two pictures you drew. Which one gives you a better feeling about yourself? (Circle your answer.)

The first one   The second one

What can you use from the second situation to help you do better in the first situation?

_____

How might you change what you do in situations like the first one, to help you procrastinate less in the future?

_____

21 break it down!

for you to know

Understandably, if a task seems overwhelming, you may be reluctant to tackle it. Breaking down what seems like a big undertaking into "bite-size" pieces can help make almost any task more manageable.

Daphne, a sixth-grader, would wait until the last minute to complete her school projects. She'd then rush through and do a poor job on the project just to get it done.

Daphne's mom decided to help Daphne learn how to break a project down into steps so that it didn't seem so overwhelming. The next time Daphne had a project—in science—she and her mom sat down with a calendar and put the final due date on the calendar. Then, they discussed the project and determined what steps were involved. Daphne's mom helped her estimate how long each step would take, and they entered these short-term due dates on the calendar. Daphne and her mom then wrote out logical directions for each step of the project. Daphne now had written directions for each part of the project and a date by when it should be done. This made the project feel more manageable for Daphne, and she was no longer stressed out by thinking that she had to do the entire project at once.

When Daphne turned in her science project, she received a much better grade than she had on projects on which she'd rushed. She felt very proud of her accomplishment, and in the future she used the same process for all her school projects.

for you to do

Following are the directions Daphne's science teacher had written for the project.

Choose any animal from the animal kingdom. Create a colorful poster and correctly label the animal based on its kingdom, phylum, class, order, family, genus, and species. Be sure to put the "common" name for the animal at the top. This project is due on March 21.

Daphne and her mom broke down the project into the following steps. Label them 1 to 7 according to the order in which you think they should be done, then give a reasonable due date for each. Keep in mind that some steps will take longer than others. (Assume that the project was assigned on March 1.)

Step	Date Due
_____ Label the animal.	_____
_____ Turn in the project.	March 21
_____ Do research.	_____
_____ Draw the animal on the poster.	_____
_____ Choose an animal.	_____
_____ Color the poster.	_____
_____ Write the animal's "common" name.	_____

more to do

Breaking down a project involves figuring out what the steps are. The first step is usually the most important and sometimes the hardest to get started on.

Try to figure out the very first thing you'd need to do to get started on each of the following projects. Then ask friends or your parents what *they* think would be the first step and compare your answerw. Do you seem to be on the right track? The first one has been done for you, as an example.

Painting a Room

Step 1: *Determine what color you want the room to be.*

Cleaning Your Bedroom

Step 1: _____

Doing a Math Assignment

Step 1: _____

Washing the Dog

Step 1: _____

Writing a Book Report

Step 1: _____

Washing the Dishes

Step 1: _____

Completing a History Project

Step 1: _____

for you to know

In life, sometimes the things you need to do will be too much for you to handle on your own. This is true whether you have weakness in executive functioning or not—no one can do it all and never need help. When a task seems overwhelming, seek the help of a trusted adult or peer. A trusted adult is one who knows you and has your best interest in mind. Your parent, a favorite teacher, a counselor, or even a friend's parent can be a trusted adult.

Zach, a seventh-grader, had always struggled in school. He believed that his trouble with starting assignments and completing them on time was due to his sometimes just not understanding the assignment.

Zach also had difficulty doing chores. He didn't like that his parents always had to remind him to get his chores done.

Zach decided that he needed help. He talked to his school counselor, who recommended that he create a list of people who could help him with the different tasks or assignments he needed to do each day. Zach wrote a list that included both adults and peers he could go to when he needed support. Zach's list of support people included his mom, for when he needed help on math; his friend Tom, for keeping up with his science notes; his grandmother, for help with his chores at home; and his girlfriend, Elizabeth, for helping him proofread his English papers.

for you to do

Write the name of a different trusted adult (or peer) in each of the fingers of the following outline of a hand.

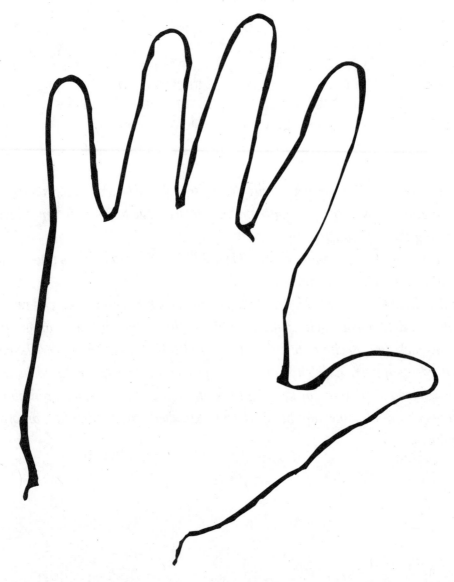

This "helping hand" is a resource you can use to identify five people who are able to help you with tasks you need to complete. In the following spaces, list all the areas in which each of these five people can help you. Try to include tasks you often procrastinate on that you listed in activity 20, "Procrastination Problems."

Name of trusted adult (or peer): _____

Areas or tasks this person can help me with:

_____

_____

Name of trusted adult (or peer): _____

Areas or tasks this person can help me with:

_____

_____

Name of trusted adult (or peer): _____

Areas or tasks this person can help me with:

_____

_____

Name of trusted adult (or peer): _____

Areas or tasks this person can help me with:

_____

_____

Name of trusted adult (or peer): _____

Areas or tasks this person can help me with:

_____

_____

more to do

List three tasks you think you might need help with in the next month.

1. _____

2. _____

3. _____

When you need to do these tasks, you can ask for help in the most appropriate way by following these steps before approaching someone on your list:

1. **Try everything you can before asking for help.** Don't immediately ask for help before trying to do the task yourself first.

2. **Admit to yourself that you need help.** This can be hard to do, but no one expects you to know everything or to do everything by yourself. Remind yourself that it's okay to need help.

3. **Decide exactly what you need help with.** If you can do part of the task but not other parts, do what you can and then get help with the rest.

4. **Locate the correct person to help.** Your mom might be able to help you with math, but not science. You wouldn't ask your teacher to help with washing your dog. Make sure you find the person who can best help with what you need help with.

Getting up the nerve to ask for help can be a challenge. But if you ask politely, most people will be willing to help you. Try to be respectful when asking for and when receiving advice or help. Do your best to listen and follow directions so that the person feels helpful—this may make the person feel more inclined to help you in the future, should you ask again.

Finally, take away the lesson. Observe the way in which the person helps you, or keep in mind what the person tells you, so that the next time you need to do the same task, you'll have the skills to do it alone.

You were born into a digital world. You may encounter TVs, computers, cell phones, and other technological devices on a daily basis. These devices, which bombard us with information from many different sources, can cause teens with difficulties in the area of attention to have an even shorter attention span.

Jamal, an eleventh-grader, spent several hours a day texting his friends. He texted about school, teachers, what he was watching on TV, or what he was eating for dinner. He texted his parents about his plans for the night; he texted his teachers about his assignments. He texted about practically everything.

Jamal had a tablet too, and he used it to do many things. He played games on it, watched movies on it, and messaged his friends on it.

Last but not least, Jamal often sat in front of the TV while working on his homework. His mom would tell him to shut off the TV so he could focus on his work, but he ignored her.

Teens today are comfortable using technology that adults seem to have trouble navigating. However, many teens don't realize that trying to split their attention too much can cause them to have issues with focusing on the things that are important. Learning to "single task" can help you improve your ability to do what you need to do. Technology is great, but it needs to be kept in check and used in moderation.

for you to do

Using check marks, indicate which of the following technological devices you own or have access to. If you have a device not listed, add it to the list. Then, keep track of how much time you spend using each of these devices per day for one week.

Type of Device	Own or Have Access To (✓)	Hours per Day Used						
		Mon	Tue	Wed	Thu	Fri	Sat	Sun
Cell phone								
MP3 player								
Tablet (e.g., Kindle, Galaxy, iPad)								
Desktop computer								
Laptop computer								
Television								
DVD/Blu-ray player								
Radio								
Video game system								
Handheld PDA (e.g., iPod Touch)								

Is anyone in your life concerned about your use of these technological devices? If so, who?

_____

_____

How might these technological devices interfere with your ability to pay attention to important tasks? (For example, do you text your friends when you should be doing chores or homework?)

_____

_____

List any ideas you can come up with for limiting your use of these devices.

_____

_____

_____

_____

more to do

Spend several hours (or even a whole day) without your technological devices. Then answer the following questions.

On a scale of 0 to 10 (0 = extremely easy; 10 = extremely hard), how hard was it for you to spend time without your technological devices? (Circle your answer.)

0   1   2   3   4   5   6   7   8   9   10

What made this experience easy or hard?

_____

_____

Why do you believe that these devices are important in your life?

_____

_____

How might your life be different if you didn't have these devices?

_____

_____

List the technological devices you're willing to use less frequently.

_____

_____

What constructive tasks will you use the extra time you have freed up for? (For example, doing homework or chores.)

_____

_____

delayed gratification 24

for you to know

Gratification is getting what you want. Teens with difficulty in the area of attention will often do what they *want* to do before what they *need* to do because it's more fun, interesting, or rewarding. This is called "instant gratification" (getting what you want right away), which is the opposite of "delayed gratification" (getting what you want later).

Many years ago, some psychologists did an experiment with children. In that experiment, individual children were told that an experimenter would give them a marshmallow and then leave the room for a while. The children were told that if they could wait to eat the marshmallow until the experimenter came back into the room, they'd get another marshmallow. If they couldn't wait, they'd get only the one marshmallow. Some children ate the marshmallow before the experimenter came back. However, some children were able to wait. Years later, the experimenters followed up on the children (who were now adults) and found that the ones who had waited for the extra marshmallow did much better in school and were more successful in their jobs.

for you to do

Think about the things that you often end up doing in spite of the fact that you know you shouldn't (things like eating the marshmallow, in the experiment described above). Let's call those "want" activities. We'll call the things that you should be doing instead (things like waiting for the experimenter to return) "need" activities.

List several "want" activities and the "need" activities they sometimes keep you from doing.

Want Activities   Need Activities

Example: **playing video game** _____ instead of _doing chores_ _____

_____ instead of _____

_____ instead of _____

_____ instead of _____

_____ instead of _____

_____ instead of _____

_____ instead of _____

_____ instead of _____

_____ instead of _____

_____ instead of _____

_____ instead of _____

more to do

Learning to manage your "want" and "need" activities by yourself can be hard. One of the best ways to get a "need" activity done is to use a "want" activity as a reward. Just like the kids in the experiment with the marshmallows, if you can learn to put off doing "want" activities in order to do "need" activities, you'll get more of what you want.

Use the following chart to set up rewards for finishing the activities you need to do.

If I Do This...	Then I Get to Do This...
Example: **wash the dishes**	**Watch my favorite TV show**

25 the center of attention

for you to know

Sometimes, teens with weakness in executive functioning can have a hard time focusing and paying attention. Also, they sometimes can't seem to reduce the distractions in their environment (for example, turn off the TV when it's time to do homework) or say no to their craving for stimulation. Learning to quiet your mind and focus your attention is a good skill to practice from time to time.

Henry, an eighth-grader, was always wound up and on the go. He'd get an idea and immediately take off with it. If someone suggested driving anywhere, in less than a minute Henry would be in the car, ready to go.

Henry also couldn't filter out distractions. If he was in a room and saw a movement in the hallway, he'd look to see what it was. If someone started watching TV in the next room, he'd race out there to see what was on.

Needless to say, it was nearly impossible for Henry to get anything done. His teachers complained that he turned in his assignments half done, if at all. His parents couldn't get him to complete chores because he was so easily distracted by outside noises or the TV. How could Henry ever be able to get things done if he could never pay attention?

for you to do

For this exercise, you'll need to find a place and time to sit for about ten minutes without being interrupted. You'll also need a timer.

Set the timer for ten minutes. During this time, just sit quietly (perhaps in a comfortable chair) and let your attention wander around your surroundings. Notice what your attention wanders to, but don't try to shift your attention or focus on any one thing. Let your attention settle where it wants to, and let it move on when it's ready. When the ten minutes are up, write down all the things you saw or heard that caught your attention.

_____

_____

_____

_____

_____

_____

Were there some things that seemed to hold your attention longer than others? If so, what were they?

_____

_____

Why do you think those things held your attention longer than others?

_____

_____

_____

more to do

Training your attention takes time and effort, but you can do it. Just like learning to do anything, it takes practice.

1. Sit in the same place as in the previous exercise. Set your timer for ten minutes. This time, however, once your attention settles on something try to keep it there for as long as you can.

2. Mentally note as many details and qualities of the object of your attention as you can, whether it's something you see, something you hear, or both. Try to identify at least five characteristics.

3. Once you've explored all the characteristics of whatever you're focusing on, let your mind wander to the next thing you notice in your environment. Repeat the process until your ten minutes are up.

The first time you do this exercise, answer the following two questions.

1. How many things caught your attention this time? Name them.

_____

_____

_____

_____

_____

_____

_____

2. Was this fewer or more things than in the previous exercise? (Circle your answer.)

Fewer   More

Try to practice this exercise every day for a week—once you've practiced it several times, see whether you can get your attention to focus on *one* thing in your environment for the entire ten minutes, then answer the following questions.

Were you able to focus on *one* thing for the entire ten minutes? (Circle your answer.)

Yes   No

What did you do to try to block out other sights or sounds and focus on just one thing?

_____

_____

_____

_____

After you've practiced for ten minutes every day for a week, increase the length of the exercise to fifteen minutes every day for a week, then twenty minutes every day for a week (or longer if you like), and soon you'll be much better at focusing your attention when doing almost anything.

26 improving your working memory

for you to know

Your *working memory* is where you store information that you plan to use or work with very soon. For instance, when you look up a phone number and keep it in your head or repeat it to yourself until you dial it, you're using your working memory. Even though some people have naturally better abilities in this area, anyone can improve their working memory through practice. Being able to recall lists and other information when needed is a beneficial skill to have.

Although Kristen did pretty well in elementary school, when she got to middle school, she started to struggle with homework assignments. Many times she'd forget to bring work home. If she did bring work home, she'd forget to do it or forget to turn it in.

Kristen also had a hard time following directions that contained more than two steps. For example, if her dad told her, "Clean your room and do the dishes after you finish your homework," she'd do her homework but forget to do the other things. When one day the school informed Kristin that she couldn't go on the class field trip because she had forgotten to get her permission slip signed, Kristen got very upset.

Testing by the school psychologist revealed that Kristen had weakness in the area of working memory. After Kristen began practicing memory tests on a regular basis, she got much better at remembering her responsibilities.

for you to do

On the next page is a list of words. Study the list for one minute and try to memorize it. Then come back to this page and write down all the words you remember.

_____   _____   _____

_____   _____   _____

_____   _____   _____

_____   _____   _____

_____   _____   _____

_____   _____   _____

_____   _____   _____

Your first attempt may not be very successful; however, if you practice this exercise once a week for several weeks, you may find that you get better at remembering lists. While just rereading and practicing this list will help you remember these specific words, knowing that our brains work best with images could be even more helpful to you. One way to remember a list is to create a crazy image in your head that has to do with the items in the list. For example, if you had to remember a head of lettuce for your mom, try picturing her with lettuce where her head should be. This also relates to another suggestion, which is to use specific body parts as a way to recall a list of items. Picturing putting milk on your feet and butter on your knees will surely create an unforgettable image of what you need to pick up at the grocery store.

Word List

Cat	Pliers	Green
Utah	Wrench	Washington
Orange	Horse	Grape
Dog	Kentucky	Plum
Virginia	Pear	Black
Banana	Hiccup	Screwdriver
Red	Pig	Red
Purple	Wisconsin	Bug
Hammer	Monkey	Apple
Quack	Saw	Down

more to do

Chunking is breaking large amounts of information into chunks, to make it easier to remember. For example, you can more easily recall a group of nine items later if you look at it as three groups of three, or as a group of four and a group of five. You can chunk in any way you like; there's no right way or wrong way to chunk anything. However, you'll be more likely to remember something if you can chunk it in a way that has some sort of personal meaning. For example, you might use the letters of your name to remember a list of items you need from the grocery store.

Do the following exercise the same way you did the previous one. This time, however, the information has been "chunked" for you. Then compare the results of this exercise with the results of the previous exercise to see whether chunking helped you remember more words.

_____   _____   _____

_____   _____   _____

_____   _____   _____

_____   _____   _____

_____   _____   _____

_____   _____   _____

_____   _____   _____

_____   _____   _____

Again, the more you practice chunking, the better you'll get at it. Try different ways of chunking to see which works best for you. You might put items into categories (like those in the following word list) or in alphabetical order, for example.

Word List

Animals	**Tools**	**Colors**
Cow	Socket wrench	Blue
Donkey	Drill	Yellow
Snake	Awl	White
Bird	Tape measure	Brown
Lizard	Vise	Violet

States	**Fruits**	**Random Words**
Texas	Orange	Baby
Alaska	Strawberry	Car
Vermont	Grapefruit	Oink
Wyoming	Kiwi	Lawnmower
Florida	Peach	Tomorrow

for you to know

"Mnemonic" (nee-MON-ik) comes from the Greek *mnemonikos* and means "of or pertaining to memory." Any tip or trick you use to help you remember a list or other information is a *mnemonic device*. Mnemonic devices can come in very handy when you need to memorize a shopping list, a series of events (maybe for a history test), a sequence of steps, or just about anything else. Another name for the technique of using mnemonic devices is *mnemonics*.

"Roy G. Biv." "Please excuse my dear Aunt Sally." "My very excited mother just served us noodles." Do you know any of these sayings? These are mnemonic devices you may have been taught to help you remember certain bits of information. Because they're catchy, they're easy to remember and therefore easy to recall when the time is right.

Mnemonic devices can take many different forms. "Roy G. Biv" is an *acronym*, in which each letter stands for a word. It helps us remember the colors of the rainbow: red, orange, yellow, green, blue, indigo, violet. "Please excuse my dear Aunt Sally" and "My very excited mother just served us noodles" are *acrostics*, in which the first letter of each word stands for another word. "Please excuse my dear Aunt Sally" helps us remember mathematical order of operations: parentheses, exponents, multiply, divide, add, subtract. "My very excited mother just served us noodles" helps us remember the planets: Mercury, Venus, Earth, Mars, Jupiter, Saturn, Uranus, and Neptune. An example of a *rhyming mnemonic* is "I before E except after C or sounded as A, as in 'neighbor' and 'weigh,'" which helps us remember a rule of spelling. An example of a *song mnemonic* is the ABC song you learned to help you remember the letters of the alphabet. Mnemonics helps you improve your working memory by allowing you to retain information for longer periods.

for you to do

Create acronyms, acrostics, rhymes, or songs to help you remember the following lists. If you can make your mnemonic device somehow related to the subject, it may be easier to recall when the subject comes up. For example, you might incorporate the names of the presidents into a song about the White House.

The First Ten Presidents of the United States

George Washington, John Adams, Thomas Jefferson, James Madison, James Monroe, John Quincy Adams, Andrew Jackson, Martin Van Buren, William Henry Harrison, John Tyler

_____

_____

_____

_____

The First Ten of the Fifty States in Alphabetical Order and Their Capitals

Alabama (Montgomery), Alaska (Juneau), Arizona (Phoenix), Arkansas (Little Rock), California (Sacramento), Colorado (Denver), Connecticut (Hartford), Delaware (Dover), Florida (Tallahassee), Georgia (Atlanta)

_____

_____

_____

_____

The Continents

Africa, North America, South America, Asia, Europe, Antarctica, Australia

_____

_____

_____

_____

Fifteen Items to Buy at the Grocery Store

Milk, eggs, hamburger, buns, ketchup, soda, bananas, butter, doughnuts, dish soap, shampoo, toilet paper, dog food, paper plates

_____

_____

_____

_____

more to do

Researchers have found that music and memory are very strongly connected. Think about how quickly you can recognize a song that you've heard many times before—you probably only need to hear a few notes. In addition, once you know what song it is, you can probably remember all or almost all the words. Advertisers take advantage of this connection by using jingles to make things stick in people's heads.

Now think of a task that you need to remember to do. It could be a chore, an assignment, or anything else important. Use words and ideas related to that task to create a short song or jingle to help you remember. Use whatever style of music works (from rap to country), but keep it catchy and short.

Jingle Style: _____

Jingle Copy:

_____

_____

_____

_____

_____

_____

_____

for you to know

Knowing how your brain learns things can help you with many different activities. Some teens have brains that learn best by seeing or hearing information. Others have brains that learn best by doing things. Using some "tricks" to train your brain in a way that it will remember things easily will save you a lot of time and effort.

Much of the time, fourteen-year-old Laura struggled to remember all the things that she needed to remember. Most days there was something that she forgot to do. Finally, she became frustrated with how much she forgot. She decided to make an appointment with her school counselor. Over the course of several meetings, her counselor taught Laura some tricks for improving her memory. With practice, Laura became much better at remembering things. Her mom even commented on how good her memory had become. Laura's grades improved because she could remember to complete and turn in her assignments.

for you to do

People remember information better when it's presented in a way that matches their learning style. Visual learners tend to remember things they see, auditory learners tend to remember things they hear, and tactile learners tend to remember things they do.

Following are six examples of memory tricks, two for each learning style. Put a check mark next to three you plan to try.

visual memory tricks

☐ **Start a tradition.** Place an object you wouldn't expect to see where you usually put something you have a hard time remembering to take with you. For example, if you usually leave your completed homework on your desk and forget to take it to school, put an object you wouldn't usually see, like a stuffed animal, on your desk to remind you. When you see that object, you'll remember your homework.

☐ **Use color.** Color code those things you have to remember. For example, on your calendar color all appointments green and all assignments yellow. This will make it easier both to identify things and to remember them.

auditory memory tricks

☐ **Create a song.** Take whatever you need to remember and make a song about it. For example, change the words to a well-known song to help you remember a shopping list.

☐ **Use verbal reminders.** Talk out loud so that you hear and remember. For example, as you put your boots in the closet, say to yourself, "I'm putting my boots in the closet."

tactile memory tricks

☐ **Make it a habit.** Have a place for everything and keep everything in its place. For example, if you take your cell phone to school, when you come home always put your cell phone on the same table, and if you pick it up to use it, put it back afterward.

☐ **Work your body.** Start at your toes and work your way up, using parts of your body to help you remember things. For example, if you have to remember to buy stamps and chicken fingers, think about stamping on a chicken's fingers. Silly is good!

more to do

Over the next few days, or for the next few things you need to remember, try each of the memory tricks you selected in the previous exercise and then answer the following questions.

Which trick or tricks seemed to work the best?

_____

_____

In what areas of your life did you use these memory tricks?

_____

_____

In the following space, write any other memory tricks that you can come up with in addition to the ones you've already tried. Try to incorporate what worked best for you about those tricks, whether it's a visual, auditory, or tactile element.

_____

_____

_____

_____

_____

_____

_____

letter to your future self

for you to know

Sometimes you may think that the way things are right now is the way they'll always be. Stepping outside yourself and wondering how things might change, however, is important to setting and achieving goals. Dreaming about or imagining the future by asking "What if…?" can generate ideas that lead to goals.

Nick, eighteen, was feeling very frustrated. While he'd tried several times to make changes in his life, he wasn't able to maintain them. In a last-ditch effort, he asked his older brother, David, to help him.

David sat with Nick and had him write down all the things he wanted to change about his life. Then, together, they wrote down what Nick might have to do to make those changes happen. They listed some people who might help Nick along his way. Finally, they made a checklist that Nick could use to keep himself on track.

Eventually, Nick was behaving in a way that allowed him to get the things he wanted, and he felt much better about himself and his future.

for you to do

Write a letter to your future self. In the letter, tell yourself what you see yourself doing in five to ten years. Try to include all areas of your life (work, school, family, hobbies, relationships, and so on).

Dear _____,

Here's what I see for you in the future:

_____

_____

_____

_____

_____

_____

_____

_____

_____

Sincerely,

_____

more to do

The things you wrote about in your letter could be called your dreams for the future. Your dreams for the future are things you'd like to see happen someday. The difference between a *dream* and a *goal* is that a dream doesn't have a plan to it. When you put a plan to a dream—when you identify the steps you'd need to take to make that dream a reality—it becomes a goal. Sometimes we need assistance in putting a plan to a dream.

List the dreams you wrote about in the letter.

_____

_____

_____

What steps would you need to take to turn these dreams into realities?

_____

_____

_____

Name the people in your life who can help you take these steps.

_____

_____

What other things do you need to have or work on to accomplish these steps?

_____

_____

_____

30 STICK to it!

for you to know

Imagine that your life is a ship, and you're the captain. Not too long ago, you weren't sure where you wanted to take this ship, so you were kind of sailing aimlessly, going wherever the wind took you. Now you've decided on some destinations (your goals). But imagine that ships like this one don't have an electronic navigation system. So how will you get to where you want to go? Well, you're the captain! You need to plot a course. And to maintain your course, especially when the sea gets rough and the weather gets scary, you need to keep steering the ship in the right direction until you reach your destination. Only when you set goals for yourself and stick to your plan can you achieve the things you want in life.

Learning how to set and achieve goals is a skill that requires the use of several other executive skills. You need to be able to think about who you are and what you want, organize your thoughts, manage your time, and initiate and sustain your efforts in the direction of your goal. Learning and using the mnemonic STICK will help you become more proficient in this skill. STICK stands for Specifics, Time line, I can do it, Calculable, and Know your limits.

S—Specifics. In order to set a goal, you need to have a specific end in mind. Just saying "Someday I'll do something about this" isn't enough. You need to spell out exactly what it is that you want. For example, does your goal involve certain people, places, or things? How exactly will you go about achieving it?

T—Time line. Goals have to have a time line; otherwise they're just lofty dreams. While it's great to daydream about what your future may look like, unless you decide on a time by which your goals need to be met, those dreams will remain just that.

I—I can do it. Setting goals that you can't possibly reach is more dangerous than setting no goals at all. For example, setting a goal to be able to drive before age sixteen is just not a good idea, because the law says that people under the age of sixteen can't get a license.

C—Calculable. A goal is calculable if it's worded in a way that allows you to objectively measure your progress. If your goal is vague or abstract, like "To do better in school," think of signs that would show you're moving toward or have reached your goal. "To get Bs in at least three of my classes this semester" is a calculable goal.

K—Know your limits. Setting a goal that would be very hard for you to achieve will only set you up for failure. For example, the goal of being able to jump high enough to touch the ceiling is just plain impossible for many people. However, a goal that doesn't require much effort or stretch your abilities is not very meaningful for your personal growth. There has to be a middle ground.

for you to do

Studies have shown that people who write down and track their goals are much more likely to reach them. That means that you can give yourself the best chance of turning your dreams into reality by putting your goals down on paper.

Close your eyes for a few minutes and picture the future you wrote about in the previous activity. Use all your senses to imagine where you are and what you're doing. Open your eyes and list what you saw for yourself.

_____

_____

_____

_____

Using this information, you'll now write a STICK goal for yourself. Write down as much as you can about one thing that you saw yourself doing.

S—Specifics

It helps to start your goal with the words "I will." State your goal in positive terms—steer clear of negative words like "not."

I will _____

T—Time line

When do you expect to have this done?

_____

I—I can do it

Is this something you can really do? (Circle your answer.)

Yes   No   Maybe

If your answer is yes, go to the next step. If your answer is no, why not? What would you have to change about your goal to turn a no or a maybe into a yes? Go back and revise your specifics or your time line until you feel confident that you can meet this goal.

C—Calculable

How will you know when you've reached this goal?

_____

K—Know your limits

Think like Goldilocks: not too hard, not too easy, but just right. Does this goal represent a stretch for you, but not too much of a stretch? (Circle your answer.)

Yes   No   Maybe

If your answer is yes, congratulations—you have your STICK goal. If your answer is no, why not? What would you have to change about your goal to turn a no or a maybe into a yes? Go back and revise your specifics or your time line until this goal is a challenge, but a reasonable one.

more to do

While there's no definite cutoff between "short term" and "long term," generally short-term goals are those that can be accomplished in less than a year. This means that the goal you wrote in the previous exercise is probably a long-term goal. Now, using the same procedure, write a short-term goal. It could be something as simple as saving enough money to purchase a modestly priced present for a friend or loved one.

my short-term goal

S—Specifics

What exactly what will you do?

I will _____

T—Time limit

When will you do it by? (should be less than a year) _____

I—I can do it

Is this goal realistic? (Circle your answer.)

Yes   No   Maybe

If your answer is yes, go to the next step. If your answer is no, why not? What would you have to change about your goal to turn a no or a maybe into a yes? Go back and revise your specifics or your time line until you feel confident that you can meet this goal.

C—Calculable

How will you determine when you've reached your goal?

_____

K—Know your limits

Would meeting this goal be a stretch for you, but not too much of a stretch? (Circle your answer.)

Yes   No   Maybe

If your answer is yes, congratulations—you have your short-term STICK goal. If your answer is no, why not? What would you have to change about your goal to turn a no or a maybe into a yes? Go back and revise your specifics or your time line until this goal is a challenge, but a reasonable one.

121

31 if at first you don't succeed

for you to know

While sometimes your plans will work out great, other times you may fall short of your goals. When this happens, you should rally your forces and try again. Just because you didn't achieve your goal the first time is no reason to give up on it completely. You can always get back on the wagon.

Wendy, sixteen, spent a lot of time working on her executive skills. She practiced managing her daily activities and organizing her materials. She focused on improving her memory. She even started setting goals for herself. However, try as she might, she just couldn't seem to achieve some of her short-term goals. For example, she had set herself a goal of exercising six days every week for a whole year, but after only a month, she'd started finding excuses: First, she convinced herself that she just had way too much homework to do and didn't have time to work out. Then she thought, I'm not getting fitter anyway, so why bother?

Wendy's dad noticed that she wasn't following through on the goals she'd set for herself, and he sat her down one day to talk about this. He said that she seemed to be sabotaging her workout goal by making excuses for why she couldn't work out. Together, Wendy and her dad examined her goal. It turned out that working out six days a week was not a very realistic goal for Wendy, based on all the other commitments she had. So Wendy revised her goal—from working out six days a week to working out three days a week. She also gave herself permission to feel okay about missing a workout if something came up.

Wendy was consistently able to work out two or three days a week, even with her other commitments. She noticed that not only was she happier about working out when her goal was more realistic, but she did seem to be getting fitter, and other areas of her life were coming together as well.

for you to do

Think about all the activities you've completed in this book. Which ones were less than successful for you?

_____

_____

_____

Write down why you think you were unsuccessful with these activities.

_____

_____

_____

List the names of people in your life who could help you be more successful with these activities if you were to repeat them. You may want to refer to activity 22, "Helping Hand."

_____

_____

Write down one activity you plan to try again with the help of one or more of these people.

_____

_____

_____

Explain what you'll do differently this time.

_____

_____

_____

more to do

Look up the word "sabotage" in the dictionary, and write the definition here.

_____

How do you think you might have sabotaged the activities in this book that didn't turn out the way you'd planned?

_____

_____

Discuss with a trusted adult what you might have done differently to help these activities turn out the way you'd planned, or what you can try next time. Write that person's advice here.

_____

_____

Write down some ways you might have put yourself down or "beaten yourself up" about not doing well on some of the activities in this book.

_____

_____

Being gentler and more encouraging toward yourself will allow you to accomplish more because you'll end up feeling more positive about yourself and what you do.

How could you be more gentle with yourself and encourage yourself to try these activities again?

_____

_____

Sharon A. Hansen, MSE, NBCT, is a professionally licensed school counselor in Berlin, WI. She has a bachelor's degree in developmental psychology from the University of Wisconsin-Oshkosh, and a master's degree in education with an emphasis in school counseling from the same institution. Hansen is also a National Board Certified School Counselor, and belongs to the Wisconsin School Counselor Association (WSCA) and the American School Counselor Association (ASCA). She lives in Oshkosh, WI.

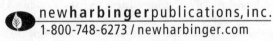

FROM OUR PUBLISHER—

As the publisher at New Harbinger and a clinical psychologist since 1978, I know that emotional problems are best helped with evidence-based therapies. These are the treatments derived from scientific research (randomized controlled trials) that show what works. Whether these treatments are delivered by trained clinicians or found in a self-help book, they are designed to provide you with proven strategies to overcome your problem.

Therapies that aren't evidence-based—whether offered by clinicians or in books—are much less likely to help. In fact, therapies that aren't guided by science may not help you at all. That's why this New Harbinger book is based on scientific evidence that the treatment can relieve emotional pain.

This is important: if this book isn't enough, and you need the help of a skilled therapist, use the following resource to find a clinician trained in the evidence-based protocols appropriate for your problem.

Real help is available for the problems you have been struggling with. The skills you can learn from evidence-based therapies will change your life.

Matthew McKay, PhD
Publisher, New Harbinger Publications

new harbinger
CELEBRATING
40 YEARS

**If you need a therapist, the following organization
can help you find a therapist trained in cognitive behavioral therapy (CBT).**

The Association for Behavioral & Cognitive Therapies (ABCT) Find-a-Therapist
service offers a list of therapists schooled in CBT techniques. Therapists listed are
licensed professionals who have met the membership requirements of ABCT
and who have chosen to appear in the directory.
Please visit www.abct.org and click on *Find a Therapist*.

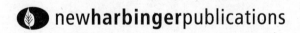